Guidelines on
Subject
Access
to Microcomputer Software

AD HOC SUBCOMMITTEE ON SUBJECT ACCESS TO

MICROCOMPUTER SOFTWARE, SUBJECT ANALYSIS COMMITTEE

CATALOGING AND CLASSIFICATION SECTION

RESOURCES AND TECHNICAL SERVICES DIVISION

AMERICAN LIBRARY ASSOCIATION

AMERICAN LIBRARY ASSOCIATION

Chicago and London 1986

Designed by Charles Bozett

Composed by Modern Typographers of Florida, Inc.
  in Linotron 202 Times Roman

Printed on 50-pound Warren's 1854
  a pH-neutral stock, and
  bound in 10-point Carolina
  cover stock by the
  University of Chicago
  Printing Department

Library of Congress Cataloging-in-Publication Data

Guidelines on subject access to microcomputer software.

  1. Cataloging of computer programs. 2. Subject
cataloging. 3. Microcomputers—Computer programs.
I. American Library Association. RTSD/CCS ad hoc
Subcommittee on Subject Access to Microcomputer
Software.
Z695.615.G84 1986   025.3'49   86-3402
ISBN 0-8389-0452-1

Contents

Preface

During the 1984 ALA Midwinter Meeting in Washington, D.C., a need was identified for guidelines on subject access to microcomputer software to complement the new guidelines on descriptive cataloging of microcomputer software. The ALA/RTSD/CCS Subject Analysis Committee (SAC) appointed the ad hoc Subcommittee on Subject Access to Microcomputer Software, with the charge to propose guidelines on subject analysis and classification of microcomputer software.

To gain an understanding of what people think subject analysis should encompass and to learn from the experiences of those libraries already dealing with cataloging and classifying microcomputer software, the SAC ad hoc Subcommittee on Subject Access to Microcomputer Software held an open hearing at the 1984 ALA Annual Conference in Dallas. With the data gathered at that hearing plus additional discussions at the 1985 ALA Midwinter Meeting, the committee has prepared the following guidelines on subject cataloging and classification of microcomputer software.

The committee wishes to thank the members of SAC for their comments and suggestions. The committee also wishes to thank Sheila Intner, who spoke at the Dallas hearing, and the many librarians who participated in the hearing and in subsequent committee meetings.

JOAN S. MITCHELL, *Chair*
PATRICIA LUTHIN
SUSAN NESBITT
ROBERT BOYER

Summary of Guidelines

Make full use of the access provided in *Guidelines for Using AACR2 Chapter 9 for Cataloging Microcomputer Software* and the machine-readable data file (MRDF) format. (See Access in the Record.)

If using the MRDF format, use *Library of Congress Subject Headings (LCSH)* as the authority (or model) for entries in the 753 field. (See Access in the Record.)

Mainstream software in subject analysis and classification. (See Subject Analysis and Classification.)

Use the proposed form subdivision *Software*. (See Subject Analysis and Classification.)

Avoid assigning individual subject headings for the make or model of machine, programming language, or operating system used by the software. (See Subject Analysis and Classification.)

Guidelines

OBJECTIVES

The *Guidelines on Subject Access to Microcomputer Software* have been developed on the following three principles:

1. The entire record (descriptive cataloging, subject cataloging, and classification) should provide the access needed by the user.
2. Sound practices of subject analysis and classification should be followed to avoid unwieldy files and useless shelf arrangements caused by grouping materials together by form alone.
3. One must ensure that adequate subject headings and linkages exist in *Library of Congress Subject Headings,* and that Library of Congress Classification and Dewey Decimal Classification have adequate provisions for the subjects covered by microcomputer software. Where standard headings are inadequate, libraries should develop and document their own according to sound principles of subject analysis.

ACCESS IN THE RECORD

No discussion of subject analysis can take place without evaluating the access that exists in the entire record. At the open hearing on subject access to microcomputer software held at the 1984 ALA Annual Conference in Dallas, the following items emerged as desirable for access: title, author, producer, programming language, operating system, model or family of microcomputers, and topic. That it is the responsibility of the catalog to provide access to all of these is clear. Some of the items already are provided in the descriptive cataloging; others should be brought out in subject analysis and classification.

3

There are several excellent guides on descriptive cataloging of micro-computer software. The basic source is *Guidelines for Using AACR2 Chapter 9 for Cataloging Microcomputer Software.*[1] In studying it, one finds that provision has been made in the descriptive cataloging for nearly everything on the list of desirable access points except the topic of the software. For instance, the rule governing the system requirements note (Rule 9.7B15) instructs the cataloger to identify the make and model on which the software runs, the amount of memory required, the operating system, the software requirements, and the kind and characteristics of any peripherals that are needed or recommended if the information is available with the software. Information on alternate equipment also may be given in a note.

Another basic source for cataloging microcomputer software is the new machine-readable data file format.[2] The MRDF format contains provision for user access to system requirements. Any system requirements or details listed in the Technical Details Note (field 538) can be entered as access points in the 753 field, Technical Details Access to Machine-readable Data Files.

The following is a summary of developing access points to micro-computer software. Each entry should be constructed according to the *Guidelines for Using AACR2 Chapter 9* . . . and the MRDF format.

1. Title

   Use the 245 field plus the GMD "machine-readable data file" in subfield $h. Make added title entries as needed in the 740 field.

2. Author

   Use the 100 or 700 field as appropriate.

3. Producer

   Use the 710 field.

4. System requirements

   Using the 538 field, prepare a systems requirements note describing the model or family of computers, memory, peripherals, programming language, operating system, etc. Information listed in this note can be used as added entry headings in the 753 field (this field is repeatable). To avoid confusion and to give some standardization to the contents of the 753 field, the committee recommends using the form of the heading for the machine, operating system, and programming language found in *LCSH*. If the heading doesn't exist, one should be developed using similar *LCSH* headings as models. The most current headings can be found by consulting the

L.C. Subject Headings Weekly Lists.[3] By repeating the 753 field, the cataloger can provide access in an added entry to any of these details. NOTE: Whereas the description of the system requirements is a mandatory field, the creation of any or all of the added entry headings in the 753 field is local option.

5. Annotated notes
    Use an annotated note field (520) to describe packages of software, the age level, and degree of difficulty. See page 7 for local options on subject access to the contents of this field.

6. Topical subject heading
    The committee recommends that headings be assigned for the topic or genre of the software, subdivided by the free floating subdivision *Software*. The committee recommends that headings *not be assigned* for the name of the program, the name of the computer, the computer language, the operating system, or any other information described in the system requirements note (538 field). Access to this information can be provided in the 753 field. See Subject Analysis and Classification below for a detailed explanation of subject heading guidelines and Appendix I for a listing of some topical headings.

7. Classification
    Apply the same standard of classification policy to microcomputer software as applied to other materials in the collection. Mainstream the software according to the subject instead of developing accession number schemes or grouping together all software in the computer science area. See page 7 for additional discussion on classification and Appendix III for selected LC and DDC numbers that may be applied to software.

SUBJECT ANALYSIS AND CLASSIFICATION

The subject content of microcomputer software should be viewed no differently from that of other materials. Subject headings and classification should be applied according to the same criteria as for other works in the collection. A form subdivision may be added to indicate the medium of microcomputer software, but the main subject heading should indicate the subject of the material. Likewise, a standard subdivision (in the case of DDC) may be added to the class number to indicate the form, but the main class number should be determined from what the software is about rather than the fact that it is software.

There are three questions to ask about subject headings for micro-computer software in conjunction with the second objective:

1. What should be the main subject heading?
2. What form subdivision should be applied to microcomputer software?
3. How should the machine or operating system be incorporated in the subject analysis?

The main subject heading should reflect what the software is about and not the form the software takes (i.e., not *Computer programs*). The committee also recognizes a need to provide access to the genre of the software (e.g., *Adventure games* would be an appropriate subject heading for a specific adventure game). While this is not current LC practice, users have expressed the desire for such access. In all applications of subject headings, the cataloger should choose the most specific heading available.

The only heading now in *LCSH* that is appropriate as a form subdivision for microcomputer software is the free-floating subdivision *Computer programs*. Applying this subdivision to microcomputer software blurs the distinction between books containing listings of programs and the software itself. As an alternative, Hennepin County Library has adopted *Software* as the form subdivision for the actual software. The committee recommends the use of *Software* as the form subdivision for the actual software.

The committee considers the addition of a second subdivision for the machine or operating system used by the microcomputer software as local option (e.g., Topic—Form subdivision—Computer model or Operating system). The committee does not recommend separate subject entries for the machine model, operating system, or programming language. The committee also does not recommend a separate heading under *Computer software* or *Computer programs*. The application of such headings would probably create files too large to be of use in the physical card catalog, and possibly too ambiguous to be of use in the online catalog. A subject entry would not be made under the programming language in which the software is written or the operating system under which it runs for the same reason one would not routinely make an entry under the language in which a book is written. If access to certain technical details such as machine, operating system, etc., are provided in the descriptive cataloging, it is questionable whether the access should be duplicated in the subject analysis. OCLC and RLIN are planning to index the 753 field.

Certainly card sets can include this field as an access point, and it can be defined as a searchable field in many online catalogs.

The subject treatment of information found in an annotated note (520 field) is also local option. For instance, topical subject headings may be created for each type of software found in an integrated software package. The age level or degree of difficulty as stated in an annotated note may be added as a subdivision to a topical heading.

Classification of microcomputer software should not be approached any differently from the classification of the rest of the collection. To choose an accession number arrangement over LC Classification or DDC may not seem wrong when the collection is small. As the collection grows, however, ignoring the shelf arrangement reduces overall access to the material. Within LC Classification or DDC, it is important to classify the software according to topic or subject in the same manner it would be classed if it were a book. Classifying solely on the basis of form would require the user to browse through large sections of dissimilar subjects shelved together simply on the basis that they were all microcomputer software.

ADEQUACY OF STANDARD SUBJECT HEADINGS AND CLASSIFICATION

The adequacy of standard sources for subject headings and classification is an ongoing concern for catalogers dealing with all types of materials. Appendix I contains a list of current headings in *LCSH* which are useful for microcomputer software. Appendix II contains sources for developing headings for microcomputer software when those found in *LCSH* are insufficient or do not exist. As mentioned before, the *L.C. Subject Headings Weekly Lists* provide information on headings recently developed at LC and are a much timelier source than *LCSH* itself. It is expected that cataloging of 1,000 software titles by the Cataloging in Publication Project of the Library of Congress will begin in 1986, which will provide some insight into LC's handling of subject analysis and classification of microcomputer software.

In the area of classification, the complete revision of the Dewey computer science schedule (004–006) should prove very helpful to classifiers of microcomputer software.[4] For microcomputer software of general applicability, there is provision in the computer science area for arrangement by type of computer, programming language, computer model, or specific program. A standard subdivision for computer programs (regardless of form) has been included, so that classifiers may class programs with the appropriate subject and add on the form subdivision to indicate that it is a program.

REFERENCES

1. American Library Association, Committee on Cataloging: Description and Access, *Guidelines for Using AACR2 Chapter 9 for Cataloging Microcomputer Software* (Chicago: ALA, 1984).

2. A description of the OCLC implementation of the MRDF format can be found in *Machine-readable Data Files Format* (Dublin, Ohio: OCLC, 1984).

3. *L.C. Subject Headings Weekly Lists* (Washington, D.C.: Library of Congress, 1984–   ).

4. *DDC, Dewey Decimal Classification. 004–006 Data Processing and Computer Science and Changes in Related Disciplines* (Albany, N.Y.: Forest Pr., 1985).

Appendixes

I. SUBJECT HEADINGS

This is a selected list of subject headings for computer topics and equipment that may prove helpful in cataloging microcomputer software. The majority of headings are Library of Congress subject headings as found in the June 1984 cumulation of *Library of Congress Subject Headings in Microform.* Other sources are indicated as follows:

1984	*Supplement to LC Subject Headings.* 1984.
1985 List No.	*L.C. Subject Headings Weekly List No.*
HCL	Hennepin County Library. *Authority List.*

The list also contains cataloger's notes, scope notes, and definitions of headings. These are indicated as follows:

CN	Cataloger's Note
SN	Scope Note (*LCSH*)
DEF	Definition

I. HARDWARE

A. General

Computers
> SN: Here are entered works on modern electronic computers first developed after 1945. Works on present-day calculators and mechanical computers of pre-1945 vintage are entered under Calculators.

Electronic digital computers

Supercomputers (1984)
> SN: Here are entered works on machines capable of performing hundreds of millions of floating-point operations per second and

having word lengths in the order of 64 bits and main memory in millions of words.

Minicomputers
DEF: A medium-scale computer, larger than a microcomputer, offers a wide variety of capabilities and may support the use of several hundred terminals simultaneously.

Microcomputers
DEF: Small computer systems, commonly called "home computers," "personal computers," or "business computers," and distinguished largely by their internal memory, storage capacity, and price.

Portable computers (1984)
DEF: Portable microcomputer systems.

B. Specific models of computer systems on the market
CN: The following terms are *LCSH* headings that also may be used in the 753 field as a tracing for "Hardware." Headings for all sizes of computers have been included to provide a comprehensive view of the form of headings for specific machines.

Adam (Computer)
AIM 65 (Computer)
Amstrad Microcomputer (1984)
Apple computer
Apple II (Computer)
Apple II Plus (Computer)
Apple IIc (Computer) (1984)
Apple IIe (Computer)
Apple III (Computer)
Aragats computer
ARITMA computer
AT&T PC 6300 (Computer) (1984)
Atari 400 (Computer)
Atari 600XL (Computer) (1984)
Atari 800 (Computer)
Atari 800XL (Computer) (1984)
Atari 1200XL (Computer) (1984)
Atari computer
Atari XL computers (1984)
ATE 80 (Computer)
ATLAS (Computer)
ATLAS 1906A (Computer)

BBC Microcomputer
Besm computer
Burroughs B1726 (Computer)
Burroughs B3500 (Computer)
Burroughs B5700 (Computer)
Burroughs B6000 series (Computers)
Burroughs B6700 (Computer)
Burroughs B7000 series (Computers)
Burroughs D-Machine (Computer)
C.mmp (Computer)
C11-10010 (Computer)
CAP (Computer)
CBM (Computer)
CDC 3300 (Computer)
CDC 3400 (Computer)
CDC 3600 (Computer)
CDC 6000 (Computer)
CDC 6400 (Computer)
CDC 6600 (Computer)
Cellatron C8205 (Computer)
Cellatron computer
Commodore 64 (Computer)
Commodore 128 (Computer) (1985 List No. 19)
Commodore computers
Commodore Plus/4 (Computer) (1984)
COMPAQ Portable Computer
Cromenco Z-2D (Computer) (1984)
CYBER 172 (Computer)
CYBER 203 (Computer) (1985 List No. 6)
CYBER computer
DEC computers
DEC microcomputers (1984)
DEC Professional 300 series (Computers)
DEC Professional 350 (Computer)
DEC Rainbow 100 (Computer)
DECSystem-10 (Computer)
DECSystem-20 (Computer)
Denelcor HEP (Computer) (1985 List No. 4)
Dnepr computer
Dnipro computer
Dragon 32 (Computer)
Eagle computers
Electron Microcomputer (1984)

Elliott computer
EMG 830 (Computer)
Epson computers (1985 List No. 6)
Epson HX-20 (Computer) (1984)
Epson QX-10 (Computer) (1984)
Ermeth computer
ES 1010 (Computer)
ES 1020 (Computer)
ES 1030 (Computer)
ES 1033 (Computer) (1984)
ES 1045 (Computer)
ES 1050 (Computer)
ES 2420 (Computer)
Exidy Sorcerer (Computer) (1984)
FELIX C-256 (Computer)
Franklin Ace 1000 (Computer) (1984)
Franklin computer
G-machine (Computer)
Garni computer
GE 600 series (Computers)
GIER (Computer)
Heathkit H-8 (Computer)
Hewlett-Packard computers
HHC (Computer)
HP/1000 (Computer)
HP/2000 (Computer)
HP Touchscreen computers (1985 List No. 15)
Hyperion (Computer) (1984)
IBM 360 (Computer)
IBM 370 (Computer)
IBM 650 (Computer)
IBM 1130 (Computer)
IBM 1401 (Computer)
IBM 1440 (Computer)
IBM 1620 (Computer)
IBM 1800 (Computer)
IBM 3965 (Computer)
IBM 5100 (Computer)
IBM 7030 (Computer)
IBM 7040 (Computer)
IBM 7044 (Computer)
IBM 7090 (Computer)

IBM 7094 (Computer)
IBM 9000 (Computer) (1984)
IBM computers
IBM microcomputers (1984)
IBM Personal Computer
IBM Personal Computer AT (1985 List No. 4)
IBM Personal Computer XT (1984)
IBM PCjr (Computer) (1984)
IBM Portable Personal Computer (1984)
IBM series/1 (Computer)
IBM series/3 (Computer)
IBM series/32 (Computer)
IBM series/38 (Computer)
ICL 1900 (Computer)
ICL 2900 (Computer)
ICL 2903 (Computer)
ICL 2904 (Computer)
Illiac computer
INAC (Computer)
INTEL 432 (Computer)
INTEL 8048 (Computer)
INTEL 8051 (Computer)
INTEL 8080A (Computer)
INTEL 8085A (Computer)
INTEL SDK-85 (Computer)
IRIS 50 (Computer)
ISS 714 (Computer)
JOHNNIAC computer
Kaypro 10 (Computer) (1984)
Kaypro 11 (Computer) (1984)
Kaypro computers
Kiev computer
KIM-1 (Computer)
KRS 4201 (Computer)
Leo computer
Lisa computer
Lockheed SUE (Computer)
LSI 11 (Computer)
MACC-7-S (Computer)
Macintosh (Computer) (1984)
MC6800 (Computer)
MESM (Computer)

MicroAce (Computer)
Minsk computer
Mir computer
Morrow computers (1984)
Motorola computers
MSX computers (1985 List No. 9)
MU5 (Computer)
Nairi computer
NEAC 2200 (Computer)
NEC PC-8200 (Computer) (1984)
NEC PC-8201 (Computer) (1984)
NEC PC-8201A (Computer) (1984)
NSC800 (Computer)
ODRA computer
Olivetti M-10 (Computer) (1984)
Oric 1 (Computer)
Oric Atmos (Computer) (1984)
Osborne computer
Panasonic Jr-200 (Computer) (1984)
PDP-8 (Computer)
PDP-10 (Computer)
PDP-11 (Computer)
Pegasus computer
PET (Computer)
Promin' computer
RC 4000 (Computer)
RCA 301 (Computer)
ROBOTRON 300 (Computer)
ROBOTRON 4000 (Computer)
ROBOTRON 4200 (Computer)
ROBOTRON 4201 (Computer)
RPC 4000 (Computer)
S6800 (Computer)
Sanyo MBC-550 (Computer) (1984)
Sanyo MBC-555 (Computer) (1985 List No. 4)
Seac computer
Sesm computer
Setun' computer
Sharp pocket computers (1984)
Siemens BS 2000 (Computers)
Sinclair QL (Computer) (1984)
Sinclair ZX Spectrum (Computer)

Sinclair ZX80 (Computer)
Sinclair ZX81 (Computer)
Soemtrom 381 (Computer)
Sord computer
Strela computer
Swec computer
Synertek SYM-1 (Computer)
Tandem computer
Tandy 1000 (Computer) (1985 List No. 17)
Tandy 2000 (Computer) (1984)
TI 99/2 (Computer) (1984)
TI 99/4 (Computer)
TI 99/4A (Computer)
TI 99/7 (Computer)
TI CC 40 (Computer)
TI Professional computer (1984)
Timex 1000 (Computer)
Timex Sinclair 1500 (Computer)
Timex Sinclair 2000 (Computer)
Timex Sinclair 2068 (Computer)
Titan (Computer)
TMS9900 family (Computer)
TOSBAC-40 (Computer)
TRS-80 Color Computer (1984)
TRS-80 Color Computer 2 (1984)
TRS-80 computers (1984)
TRS-80 MC-10 (Computer) (1984)
TRS-80 Model 4 (Computer) (1984)
TRS-80 Model 4P (Computer) (1984)
TRS-80 Model 16 (Computer) (1984)
TRS-80 Model 100 (Computer) (1984)
TRS-80 Model I (Computer) (1984)
TRS-80 Model II (Computer) (1984)
TRS-80 Model III (Computer) (1984)
TRS-80 PC-1 (Computer) (1984)
TRS-80 PC-2 (Computer) (1984)
TRS-80 pocket computers (1984)
Univac computer
Univac 1004 (Computer)
Univac 1100 series (Computer)
Univac 1107 (Computer)
Univac 1108 (Computer)

Univac 1219 (Computer)
Ural computer
VAX-11 (Computer)
VIC 20 (Computer)
Victor 9000 (Computer)
WANG 2200 (Computer)
Wisc computer
Workslate (Computer) (1984)
Zenith Z-100 (Computer) (1984)

C.   Peripherals, memory, etc.

Computer input/output equipment
Computer interfaces
Computer output microfilm
Computer storage devices
Computer terminals
Computers—Optical equipment
Data disk drives
Data tape drives
Data tapes
Expansion boards (Microcomputers) (1984)
Light pens
Modems
Printers (Data processing systems)
Smart cards (1985 List No. 4)
Video display terminals (1984)

D.   Communication networks

Computer networks
Information networks
Local area networks (Computer networks) (1984)
Telecommunication . . .

II. SOFTWARE

A.   General

Computer programs
Computer programs—Design
Computer software (1985 List No. 1)
Debugging in computer science
Microcomputers—Programming

Programming (Electronic computers)
Structured programming (1985 List No. 10)

1. Specific types of computer programs (selected examples)
    CN: These *LCSH* headings may be used in conjunction with names of specific programs

    Compilers (Computer programs)
    Digital computer simulation (HCL uses Computer simulation)
    Integrated software (Computer programs) (HCL)
    CN: An annotated note (520 field) linking the types of programs "integrated" in the specific piece of software is an option to this heading.
    Interpreters (Computer programs)
    Teleprocessing monitors (Computer programs) (1985 List No. 16)
    Text editors (Computer programs)
    Utilities (Computer programs)

    a. Specific computer programs (selected examples)

        dBASE II (Computer program) (1984)
        LOTUS 1-2-3 (Computer program)
        SuperCalc (Computer program)
        VisiCalc (Computer program
        WordStar (Computer program)

B. Operating systems (Computers)
    DEF: A program that controls the way information is loaded into memory, the way the computer works with the information, the way information is stored on a disk, and the way the computer talks to printers and other peripheral devices.

1. Specific operating systems (selected examples)
    CN: The following are *LCSH* terms and may be used in the 753 field to designate the operating system used with a particular piece of software.

    CP/68 (Computer operating system)
    CP/M (Computer operating system)
    CP/M-80 (Computer operating system)
    CP/M-86 (Computer operating system)
    CP/M Plus (Computer operating system)
    MP/M (Computer operating system)
    MS-DOS (Computer operating system)

OS BAMOS (Computer operating system) (1984)
PC DOS (Computer operating system) (1984)
RT-11 (Computer operating system)
UNIX (Computer operating system)
VAX/VMS (Computer operating system)
Xinu (Computer operating system)

C. Programming languages (Electronic computers)

1. Specific programming languages (selected examples)
   CN: The following are *LCSH* terms which may be used in the 753 field to designate the specific programming language of a piece of software.

   AL (Computer program language) (1984)
   BASIC (Computer program language)
   C (Computer program language)
   COBOL (Computer program language)
   DATAPLOT (Computer program language) (1984)
   FORTH (Computer program language)
   FORTRAN (Computer program language)
   LOGO (Computer program language)
   PASCAL (Computer program language)
   PILOT (Computer program language)

III. APPLICATIONS

A. General

1. [Topic]—Data processing
   (DEF: Application of automation to subject)
2. [Topic]—Computer programs
   (DEF: Listings of programs or programs in general)
3. [Topic]—Software
   (DEF: The piece of software itself, disk, etc.)
4. Information storage and retrieval systems—[Topic]
5. Data base management—[Topic]

B. Art

Computer animation
Computer art
Computer drawing
   SN: Here are entered works on the use of computer graphics to create artistic designs.

Computer graphics
SN: Here are entered works on the technique for producing line drawings, including particularly engineering drawings by use of current digital computing and plotting equipment.

C. Authorship

Computer-generated literature (HCL)
Computer poetry
Computer prose (1984)

D. Business

Data base management
Electronic spreadsheets (1984)
Mailing labels—Production (HCL)
Time management
Word processing

E. Education

Computer-assisted instruction
SN: Here are entered works on automated method of instruction in which a student interacts directly with instructional materials stored in a computer.
Computer literacy
SN: Here are entered works on the ability to use and understand computer systems, including their capabilities, applications, and social implications, in order to function effectively in a computer-based society.
Computer-managed instruction
SN: Here are entered works on the use of computers to assist teachers and administrators in coordinating the instruction process, e.g., retrieving and summarizing performance records and cumulating files.
Computers—Programmed instruction
Computers—Study and teaching
Computers and children (1985 List No. 17)
Educational software (HCL)

F. Entertainment

Computer games
SN: Here are entered works on games played on a computer.
CN: The following headings are "genre headings" and are

19

not recognized in this context by *LCSH*. Use them if your collection warrants it.

Adventure games (HCL)
Arcade games (HCL)
Computer game design (HCL)
Counting games (HCL)
Educational games (HCL)
Fantasy games (1984)
Interactive fiction (HCL)
> CN: This heading refers to the new genre of electronic novels and computer literature.

Specific games, e.g., Chess—Software
Sports computer games (HCL)
War games

Games—Data processing
> SN: Here are entered works on the application of computers and data processing techniques to games in general, including recording statistics, setting up tournaments, etc.

Interactive video (1984)
Video games

G. Home applications

Menu planning (HCL)
Shopping lists (HCL)

H. Library/Information science

Acquisition of computer programs (1984)
Catalog, On-Line
Cataloging of microcomputer software (1984)
On-line bibliographic searching
On-line data processing—Downloading (1985 List No. 19)
On-line data processing—Uploading (1985 List No. 19)

I. Music

Computer composition (HCL)
> SN: Here are entered materials on the composition of computer music.

Computer music
Computer sound processing

J. Personal finance

Finance, Personal

K. Publishing

Computerized typesetting

L. Society

Computer bulletin boards
SN: Here are entered materials on computer services which function like a community bulletin board and allow a remote caller to dial a central calling place to enter and receive messages, access bulletins or notices, etc.
Computer camps
Computer crimes
Computer espionage (HCL)
Computer industry
Computer stores (1984)
Computerphobia (HCL)
Computers—Religious aspects (1985 List No. 17)
Computers—Religious aspects—Buddhism [Christianity, etc.] (1985 List No. 17)
Computers and civilization
Computers and family (1985 List No. 17)
Computers and literacy (1985 List No. 9)
Telecommuting (1985 List No. 1)

II. SOURCES FOR NEW SUBJECT HEADINGS

Bates, William. *The Computer Cookbook*. New York: Quantum Press/ Doubleday, 1984.

More than just a dictionary, this book relates general groups of terms to one another. For example, in discussing adventure games the genre is compared to fantasy games and interactive fiction.

Berman, Sanford. "Do-it-yourself Subject Cataloging: Sources and Tools," *Library Journal* 107 (April 15, 1982) 785–86.

This article does not include sources specifically for creating subject headings for computer material. Rather, it outlines an approach for creating new subject headings and cross references the "Berman" way.

Hennepin County Library. *Authority List* (1977–). Quarterly. 42x microfiche.

Includes genre headings for games, educational software, etc. Also includes new cross references for LC headings.

Hennepin County Library. *Library Bulletin*. Bimonthly.

Totally new headings, replacements to LC headings, new notes, and cross references.

L.C. Subject Headings Weekly Lists. Washington, D.C.: Library of Congress, 1984–

These lists typically include many new computer-related subject headings which have not yet appeared on fiche and do not appear in *LCSH*.

Microcomputer Index. Database Services, 1984– . Bimonthly.

The "Reader's Guide" of microcomputers provides some specific and general subject headings for software which can be used in a catalog record.

The Software Catalog: Microcomputers. New York: Elsevier, 1984.

Contains a subject and applications index and a keyword and program name index, both of which provide clues as to how the software producers describe their products and how the public may be approaching a description in the library.

Literary warrant from the packaging, documentation, reviews, etc., of the software item may also be used.

III. CLASSIFICATION

I. SOME GENERAL LC CLASSIFICATION NUMBERS

A. Electronic digital computers

QA76.6 Programming
.7 Programming languages
.73 Individual programming languages, A–Z
.8 Special computers, systems, By name, A–Z
.9 Other topics
.B84 Bulletin boards
.C64 Computer literacy
.C65 Computer simulation
.C659 Computers and children
.C66 Computers and civilization
.D3 Data base management
.S65 Software maintenance

B. Computer games. Computer simulated games. Electronic games.

GV1469.25 Individual games, A–Z.

C. Electronic data processing (Business programs)

HF5548.4 Special computers, systems, programs, By name,
A–Z. e.g., VisiCalc is .V57
.5 Programming language

D. Word processing

Z52.5 Individual programs, machines, etc., A–Z
e.g., WordStar is .W67

E. Computerized typesetting

Z253.4 By specific language or system, A–Z

II. SOME GENERAL DEWEY DECIMAL CLASSIFICATION NUMBERS

Entirely new, revised, and expanded data processing and computer science schedules have been issued by Forest Press.[1] In order to allow room for expansion and avoid the reuse of numbers, the data processing and computer science schedules have been moved from 001.6 to 004–006, and computer engineering has been moved from 621.38195 to 621.39.

The schedules provide for new topics in computer science and allow a greater degree of specificity in classifying certain topics. Of particular interest is the schedule for programs, 005.3. 005.3 is divided first by type of computer, then further divided by specific programming language, specific computer, and specific program.

The new revision also explains the use of standard subdivision 028553 with regard to computer programs. Standard subdivision 028553 and its subdivisions can be used to denote programs themselves and works about programs (regardless of form) and may be applied to any number except those already implying data processing, computer science, computer communications, or applications of these.

Some useful numbers elsewhere in Dewey that may be applied to microcomputer software include:

652.5	Word processing
658.05	Computer applications in management
789.99	Computer music
794.82	Computer games

---

1. *DDC, Dewey Decimal Classification. 004–006 Data Processing and Computer Science and Changes in Related Disciplines* (Albany, N.Y.: Forest Pr., 1985).

IV. EXAMPLES

Type: m	Bib lvl: m	Govt pub:	Lang: N/A	Source: d	Frequn: n
File: b	Enc lvl: I	Machine: a	Ctry: cau	Dat tp: s	Regulr:
Desc: a	Mod rec:	Dates: 1984,			

090		HF5548.4 $b .F698
092		005.369
245	00	Framework $h machine-readable data file
250		Version 1.1.
260		Culver City, Calif. : $b Ashton-Tate, $c c1984.
300		1 computer program on 5 computer disks ; $c 5¼ in. + $e 2 manuals (loose-leaf ; 26 cm.) + 1 quick guide + 3 templates.
500		Includes backup copy of system disk #1.
520		This "advanced business program" includes 7 interactive modes: outlining, word processing, spreadsheet, data management, graphics, DOS access, and telecommunications. [optional]
538		System requirements: IBM PC, PC XT, or compatible computer; 384K; DOS 2.0 or later; 2 360K floppy disk drives or 1 360K floppy disk drive and hard disk drive; monitor; printer, plotter, and Intel 8087 co-math processor are optional.
650	0	Word processing $x Software. [optional]
650	0	Electronic spreadsheets $x Software. [optional]
650	0	Data base management $x Software. [optional]
650	0	Telecommunication $x Software. [optional]
690	0	Integrated software $x Software.
690	0	Integrated software $x Software $x IBM Personal Computer. [optional]
710	20	Ashton-Tate.
740	01	Frame work $h machine-readable data file.
753		IBM Personal Computer. [optional]
753		IBM Personal Computer XT. [optional]

Type: m	Bib lvl: m	Govt pub:	Lang: N/A	Source: d	Frequn: n
File: b	Enc lvl: I	Machine: a	Ctry: mau	Dat tp: s	Regulr:
Desc: a	Mod rec:	Dates: 1983,			

090		GV1469.25 $b .W53
092		794.82
245	00	Witness $h machine-readable data file.
260		Cambridge, Mass. : $b Infocom, Inc., $c c1983.
300		1 program file on 1 computer disk ; $c 5¼ in. + $e interlogic reference card + booklet + facsimile newspaper page, telegram, letter, matchbook.
440	0	Infocom mystery series
520		An "advanced" interactive fiction game of logic, in which the player attempts to solve a crime, based on clues provided. [optional]
538		System requirements: Apple II+ or IIe; 32K.
650	0	Detective and mystery stories $x Software.
690	0	Interactive fiction $x Software.
690	0	Interactive fiction $x Software $x Apple II Plus (Computer). [optional]
690	0	Interactive fiction $x Software $x Apple IIe (Computer). [optional]
710	20	Infocom, Inc.
753		Apple II Plus (Computer). [optional]
753		Apple IIe (Computer). [optional]

Type: m	Bib lvl: m	Govt pub:	Lang: N/A	Source: d	Frequn: n
File: b	Enc lvl: I	Machine: a	Ctry: cau	Dat tp: s	Regulr:
Desc: a	Mod rec:	Dates: 1984,			

090		Z52.5 $b .B35
092		652.5
245	00	Bank Street writer $h machine-readable data file : $b word processor / $c Developed by the Bank Street College of Education, Franklin E. Smith and Intentional Educations, Inc.
250		Enhanced version / $b by Gordon Riggs.
260		San Rafael, Calif. : $b Broderbund Software, $c c1984.
300		3 program files on 2 computer disks; $c 5¼ in. + $e 1 manual (62 p.) + 1 "Quick start" card.
500		Original program by Gene Kusmiak.
500		Main disk includes Bank Street writer tutorial program for Apple IIe on back side; back-up disk includes tutorial program for II+ machine on its back side.
520		This is an "easy" word processing program for 5th grade to adult. [optional]
538		System requirements: Apple II+ or IIe; 64K; DOS 3.3; mouse optional (IIe only).
650	0	Word processing $x Software.
650	0	Word processing $x Software $x Apple II Plus (Computer). [optional]
650	0	Word processing $x Software $x Apple IIe (Computer). [optional]
700	10	Smith, Franklin E.
700	10	Kusmiak, Gene.
700	10	Riggs, Gordon.
710	20	Bank Street College of Education.
710	20	Intentional Educations, Inc.
710	20	Broderbund Software.
740	01	Bank Street writer tutorial $h machine-readable data file.
753		Apple II Plus (Computer). [optional]
753		Apple IIe (Computer). [optional]